The Voyage of the Gray Whale

Anin[...]
plexe[...]
trigger these journeys? What phenomena dic-
tate their paths? No one knows for certain. The
gray whale* has been making its annual pil-
grimage from summer feeding grounds in the
Arctic seas to winter breeding lagoons in Baja
California for hundreds of thousands of years.
How do new generations learn the way? And
how do they navigate the route so unerringly?
Evidence suggests that gray whales follow
contours of the bottom, at the water depths
they prefer. Movement of the sun, ocean cur-
rents, and even the taste of sediments flowing
from rivers, bays, and lagoons also assist in the
passage. Whatever the combination of navi-
gational aids, we know the gray whale's migratory route brings it within sight of land along
vast stretches of the Pacific coastline on a pre-
dictable schedule. For millions of Pacific Coast
residents and visitors, the result has been their
discovery and enjoyment of the "gentle art of
whalewatching."

*More precisely, the "California-Chukotka popula-
tion of gray whales," about which this book is written.
The coastal habits of gray whales made them the target
of whalers for centuries, resulting in the extinction
of the Atlantic gray whale and near-extinction of the
Korean stock. Today, only the California-Chukotka
population survives in substantial numbers.

Published by Sasquatch Books
1931 Second Avenue
Seattle, WA 98101
(206) 441-5555

International Standard Book Number: 0-912365-25-0.

Printed in the United States of America.

Book design by: Dustin Kahn
Cover design & illustration by: Dugald Stermer
Text illustrations: ©1983 by Pieter Arend Folkens
Maps: ©1983 by Bill Prochnow
Text written by: Ben Bennett
Technical assistance by: Steven L. Swartz
Whalewatching site data compiled by: Evelyn Wynne

The Publisher gratefully acknowledges the contributions made to this book by
the following individuals and organizations:

Jim Allan, Tia Collins, Denise Herzing, Jeff Hottowe, Tom Johnson,
Dr. Stephanie Kaza, Stan Minasian, Maxine McCloskey, Diana McIntyre,
Michael Poole, Dave Rugh, Marilyn Stansfield, Marc Webber, Donald W.
Wilkie, Birgit Winning, and Dr. Howard Wright.

American Cetacean Society, Cetacean Research Associates, Marine Mammal
Fund, Oregon State University Sea Grant College, Pacific Rim National Park,
Scripps Institute of Oceanography, U.S. National Park Service, and The Whale
Center.

Other titles from Sasquatch Books
  Northwest Best Places
  Seattle Best Places

THE OCEANIC SOCIETY
FIELD GUIDE
TO THE
GRAY WHALE

Preface

Because the migration of the gray whale brings it, at so many points, so close to the coastlines of the United States, Canada, and Mexico, it has become one of the most-observed, most-studied, and most-admired of the great whales. It is the purpose of this book to serve as a practical guide to viewing the gray whale—from land or sea, by private boat or excursion craft, on an afternoon's family outing or two-week expedition to the breeding lagoons—from points along the Pacific coastline of North America. Sections devoted to the natural history of the gray whale, to its anatomy and physiology, to its near extinction and recent resurgence, and to its annual life cycle, are included to increase your understanding of the whales and enjoyment of the whalewatching experience. But this is a guidebook, not a text. Its primary purpose is specific: to provide locations of and directions to the best whalewatching sites, from Alaska to Baja, and suggest times of the year when gray whales can be seen. Whether you are a first-time whalewatcher or life-long student of the gray whale, we believe you will find it useful.

Table of Contents

Foreword

by Keith K. Howell
Editor, OCEANS
The Oceanic Society

It was on one of the early Oceanic Society whalewatching trips off the coast of northern California (not that many years ago, really) that I first saw a gray whale close up. Its head broke the surface, and from the blowholes a spume of water and mist exploded into the air. I could sense the unseen throat as it emptied and filled with a room-full of air. Here, in the sea, was the biggest and strongest breath of life on the planet, and I had become a convert to its lore.

Since then the gray whale has experienced a renaissance, both literally and figuratively. Its numbers have increased to what some think to have been the size of the original stock. Whales have been seen swimming closer to shore with increasing frequency. And, inspired by a trusting calf, some whales have discovered that some humans mean them no harm.

That calf was born nearly a decade ago in Baja California's Laguna San Ignacio. Intrigued by the dinghies that floated beside her, and knowing no better, she swam over to a boat—and found hands reaching out to touch her. She obviously enjoyed the contact, and next year more young whales followed suit. A few years later their mothers, too, came to be petted. Recently, female whales have been seen encouraging their calves—nuzzling their young to the rubber rafts and even lifting them up to meet people. Yet these friendly whales are found only in Laguna San Ignacio. Whales who winter elsewhere have yet to learn about the "friendly people."

The changing behavior of whales is just one reason why so many descriptions in this book are qualified with an "often," a "probably," or an "it seems." Much of our information is recent, and many hypotheses remain to be tested. Each whale, too, seems to have a mind of its own; each swims to its own drummer. As they do with people, generalizations about whales quickly break down.

(For example, although many adult female gray whales become pregnant one year and give birth the next, others may have calves for three or four years in succession and then stop, for no apparent reason. Others have offspring only rarely.)

Over the millennia that man and whale have shared this planet, they have been separated by a common and impenetrable boundary. We have not entered their world, nor they ours. Only at arm's length have we tried to solve their mysteries, using only clues that come within our reach. And how mysterious and frightening we homo sapiens must seem when half of us come as killers and half as friends.

As more and more people whalewatch, and come to appreciate not only the beauty of whales but those qualities that transcend the traditional boundaries that separate us, whales will become infinitely more valuable to us alive than they ever were dead. Perhaps then we will all discover that these "extra-terrestrials," as John Lilly first called them, living with us are as exciting, extraordinary, and profound as any alien creatures science fiction ever invented.

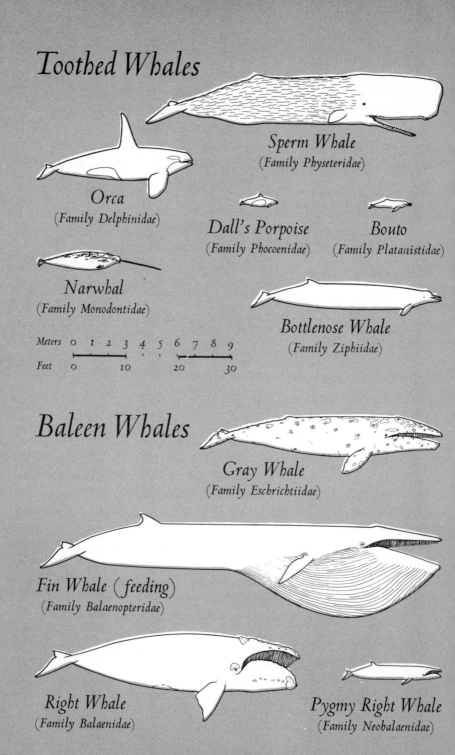

Toothed Whales

Sperm Whale
(Family Physeteridae)

Orca
(Family Delphinidae)

Dall's Porpoise
(Family Phocoenidae)

Bouto
(Family Platanistidae)

Narwhal
(Family Monodontidae)

Bottlenose Whale
(Family Ziphiidae)

Meters 0 1 2 3 4 5 6 7 8 9
Feet   0   10   20   30

Baleen Whales

Gray Whale
(Family Eschrichtiidae)

Fin Whale (feeding)
(Family Balaenopteridae)

Right Whale
(Family Balaenidae)

Pygmy Right Whale
(Family Neobalaenidae)

The Evolution of Whales

Perhaps thirty million or more years ago, and for reasons we can only guess, at least one group of land mammals re-entered the seas. Over time their bodies evolved, adapting to aquatic life. The disappearance of hind legs and gradual transformation of forelegs into pectoral fins (or flippers) are only the most obvious of many changes which took place. For all their modifications and specializations, however, they remained true mammals: air-breathing, warm-blooded animals, nursing their young on milk. Today they make up the order of marine mammals called *cetaceans*, including whales, dolphins, and porpoises.

Cetaceans are further sub-classified into Odontocetes or *Toothed whales* (including sperm whales and dolphins, for example) and Mysticetes or *Baleen whales* (of which the blue whale, humpback, and gray are representative).

Toothed whales are predatory, pursuing fish or squid which they catch with their teeth. Baleen whales are "grazers" of relatively small aquatic animals. In place of teeth, they use baleen or "whalebone" (which is actually not bone at all, but a horn-like material similar to human fingernails) to gather their food. Hundreds of fringed baleen plates hang from their upper jaw like the teeth of a comb, forming an effective sieve to filter plankton, small schooling fish, tiny shrimp-like creatures collectively called "krill," and other small sea life from the water.

Within the suborders, evolution has produced great diversity of teeth and baleen. Sperm whales have teeth only in the lower jaw, orcas (or "killer whales") in both upper and lower jaws. Fin whales have short baleen; right whale baleen is long and fine. (Gray whale baleen is short and coarse.)

Gray Whale Facts

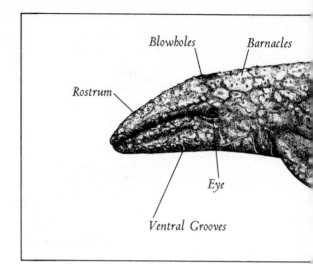

Blowholes   Barnacles

Rostrum

Eye

Ventral Grooves

Size	Mid-range for baleen whales, 35-50 ft (10.6-15 m) and 20-40 tons (18-36 metric tons). Like other baleen whales, females are slightly larger than males. Calves average 15 ft (4.5 m) at birth and weigh 1,500 lbs (680 kg).
Life Span	Average 30 to 40 years, but as long as 60 years.
Color	Slate gray, heavily mottled with white from natural pigmentation, barnacles, and barnacle scars.
Blowholes	Paired, as with all baleen whales. (Toothed whales have only one.) Approximately 8″ (20 cm) long.
Dorsal Ridge	Gray whales have no dorsal fin. Instead, a series of 6-12 "knuckles" or bumps are present along the dorsal ridge of the tail stock.
Flukes & Flippers	Tail-flukes are made of connective tissue and cartilage, approximately 12 ft (3.6 m) wide, weighing about 300-400 lbs (136-180 kg). (Whale flukes are horizontal, compared to the vertical tails of fish.) Flippers range 4-5 ft (1.2-1.5 m) long, and are supported by a skeleton derived from the forelimb of land mammals.

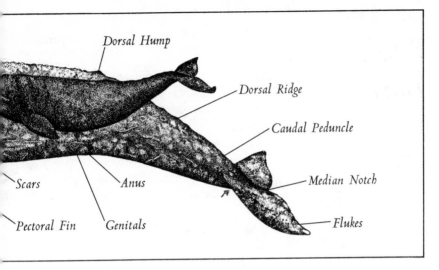

Dorsal Hump

Dorsal Ridge

Caudal Peduncle

Scars

Anus

Median Notch

Pectoral Fin

Genitals

Flukes

Swimming & Diving	Cruising speed: 2-4 kts. Top speed: approximately 10 kts. Normal dive depth: 120 ft (36 m); estimated maximum: 500 ft (150 m). Normal duration of dive: 3-5 minutes, occasionally longer than 15 minutes.
Vocalization	Like most baleen whales, gray whales vocalize in very low tones or frequencies (less than 1,000 Hz), whereas toothed whales utilize higher frequencies. Gray whales produce sounds to communicate among themselves, and to find their way in darkness and in water with limited visibility, although their "echolocation" mechanism is not understood.
Predators	Killer whales, large sharks, and man.
Parasites	Two major types of external parasites attach themselves to gray whales. Barnacles are imbedded into the hide, especially on the head, back, and tail. (A large gray whale may carry several hundred pounds of barnacles!) Cyamid lice, orange in color and up to 1" (2.5 cm) long, infest barnacle clusters and folds of skin over much of the whale's body. Gray whales also host some internal parasites, as do all whales.

Annual Life Cycle of the Gray Whale

Arctic Feeding: April–October

The Chukchi and Bering Seas lie north and south of the narrow straits separating Alaska's Seward Peninsula from the easternmost thrust of Siberia. It is in these sub-polar seas that most gray whales spend their summers, gliding through icy waters rich with nutrients. Unique among whales, they are bottom-feeders, a trait which earned them an earlier (and misleading) nickname: "mussel-digger." Although they occasionally feed on schooling fish or swarming crustaceans, small bottom-dwelling creatures called "amphipods" make up the bulk of their diet. In a typical feeding dive to the shallow sea floor, they roll onto their right sides (just like people, however, there are a few left-handers!) and suck up the bottom sediment, using their mouths like a huge vacuum cleaner. Then, with their tongue, they squeeze water and silt back out through the baleen filter, leaving behind a meal of amphipods. Although the total daily quantity of food consumed is not known, it is not uncommon to find ten or more wheelbarrow loads of amphipods in the gray's enormous, three-chambered stomach! The result by summer's end is an accumulation of six to twelve inches of oily blubber which will be an energy reserve during the winter months of migration and breeding, and nourishment for the developing calves of pregnant females.

Southern Migration: October-February

Early in October, as Arctic days shorten and the surface ice pack begins to thicken and expand southward, pregnant female grays, already well into their 12-month gestation, slip south through Alaska's Unimak Pass and begin their extraordinary annual 6,000-mile (9,600 km) journey to Baja California. Nonpregnant females, mature males, and juveniles follow over succeeding weeks. For the expectant females, the voyage is a demanding and determined one. Traveling alone or in groups of two or three, with little rest and seldom pausing to feed, they may travel 20 hours and 100 miles (160 km) each day in their urgency to reach the protected, sub-tropical lagoons in which their young are born. For the trailing whales, the journey is no less arduous. They swim in groups of up to 12 animals, and reach Baja in six to eight weeks. Males and in-season females court and mate throughout the migration, and great churning and thrashing of water frequently marks the courtship. (Because females usually give birth every other year, there are more mature males than in-season females with which to mate, resulting in competition among the males. Females may, however, mate with more than one male each year.) The migratory behavior of juveniles is less well understood. They appear to follow the adults over much of the route, but some stray from the migration, venturing away to feed, or to explore the shore or islands of Southern California. By mid-January, most females have reached the near-shore waters and lagoons of Baja California which are their destination. Stragglers continue to arrive for yet another month or more.

Annual Life Cycle of the Gray Whale

Calving Season: December–April

Most female gray whales mate one year and give birth the next, following this biennial breeding cycle from sexual maturity at the age of 6-8 years. Birth generally takes place in the shallow backwaters of Baja lagoons, although some calves are born early—during the migration itself or in near-shore waters adjacent to the Baja coast. At birth, the calves are darker than their mothers, their skin wrinkled and barnacle-free. During their time in the lagoons, they rarely venture far from their mothers, and her strong protective instincts can make her a dangerous adversary should she sense a threat to her calf's safety. (Experiencing her defense behavior firsthand, Pacific whalers gave the gray whale another of its early nicknames: "devilfish.") After two or three months, however, the calves begin to "socialize" among themselves, and to venture short distances from their mothers to explore their surroundings. Nourished by approximately 50 gallons (190 liters) a day of the mother's rich milk, a calf may gain up to 60-70 lbs (27-32 kg) each day, reaching 2-3 tons (1818-2727 kg) in weight and 18-19 feet (5.5-5.8 m) in length by the end of the winter. By mid-February, newly-pregnant females have left the lagoons for the long journey north. Adult males follow (continuing to court these females over the next several weeks), trailed by juveniles of both sexes. New mothers and their calves are last to leave, occasionally remaining as late as May or June.

Returning Home: February-July

Gray whales migrate northward in two distinct phases or "pulses," the first traveling from February to June, the second from March to July. The earliest returnees are newly-pregnant females, adult males, and juveniles. These whales generally retrace their southward trek, swimming point-to-point across bays and bights, averaging 95-100 days between Baja and Alaska. (In February, below Southern California, they encounter the last of the southbound migrants, unconcernedly tardy.) Some congregate at river mouths from northern California to Washington's Olympic Peninsula and Vancouver Island, B.C., in late March and early April, where they are frequently seen feeding on bottom organisms and swarming "mysid" shrimp. Some remain in these areas for the summer, but most continue on through Unimak Pass into the Bering Sea where they follow the receding ice edge. New mothers and their calves remain in the lagoons a month or more longer than other whales before they begin to move north. These female-calf pairs migrate close to shore, along surf lines and kelp beds, where they are frequently seen lingering for a few hours to a few days. Here it is believed that females feed, as do their calves, as they begin the transition from a milk diet to solid food. (Complete weaning occurs when the calves are 8-10 months old.) Some females arrive at the summer feeding grounds, with or without their calves, as early as June, others as late as August. There, in the abundance of the Arctic seas, the annual life cycle of the gray whale comes full circle and begins once again.

Hunting the Gray Whale

Although commercial whaling is of more recent vintage, the hunting of gray whales has been taking place for centuries. Aboriginal hunters of North America and Asia took gray whales in significant numbers, especially calves and year-lings, as they migrated along the coastlines. But it was not until the 19th century that Yankee and European whalers took up the hunt. As the stocks of commercially valuable bowhead, right, and humpback whales in the northern seas became depleted, they turned increasingly to grays to make their quotas. By 1845 they had discovered the Baja breeding grounds, and be-gan to decimate the winter population. In 1854, shore whaling began along the migratory route, and for the next 45 years some 15 shore stations from northern California to Baja California took gray whales. (Each whale yielded 25-45 barrels of oil, which sold for $27-$40 a barrel in 1855.) In 1857, Capt. Charles M. Scammon entered Laguna Ojo de Liebre, and was cred-ited with the discovery of this hidden whaling ground which now bears his name: "Scam-mon's Lagoon." For another 40 years the hunt continued, but by 1890 the population had been so reduced that whaling for grays was largely abandoned. Following the turn of the century, gray whales were for the most part ignored for some 25 years. Then, with the de-velopment of steam and diesel-powered catch boats and some recovery of the population, they became targets of the whalers once again. Gray whales did not receive complete protection until 1946, when they were declared a depleted and endangered species. Although the gray is not endangered at this time, the International Whaling Commission protects it as a "sus-tained management stock," and permits an annual take of 180 whales.

Saving the Gray Whale

Although the gray whale population was reduced to no more than a few thousand individuals in 1946, its recovery has been unmatched by any other species of great whale. (At present the population is approximately 16,000, and increasing by 2.5% annually.) This remarkable recovery is linked to the gray's unique coastal habits—habits which had previously led to its slaughter. The great coastal migration and winter gathering in Baja's breeding lagoons now worked for the survival of the species. Mates were easily located, breeding flourished, and the gray was saved. Yet even today there are threats to its continued survival. Gray whales compete with humans for the coastal habitat along virtually their entire range. They have survived eons of gradual geologic changes in the environment, but it is questionable if they can tolerate the noise, pollution, and disruption of the marine environment which are the byproducts of man's development. Gray whales, and all coastal marine species, can be assured of survival only if their habitat is managed wisely for the benefit of both whales and man. Mexico's establishment of gray whale sanctuaries in Laguna Guerrero Negro, Laguna Ojo de Liebre, and Laguna San Ignacio (the first for any cetacean) must be matched by equally sensitive treatment in other parts of the gray whale's range. Greater understanding and awareness of the interdependence of all living species will be necessary if this magnificent creature is to continue to survive.

Suggested Readings

Alaska Whales and Whaling by "Alaska Geographic" staff.

The Book of Whales by Richard Ellis.

The Delicate Art of Whale Watching by Joan McIntyre.

The Life History and Ecology of the Gray Whale by Dale W. Rice & Allen A. Wolman.

Marine Mammals, edited by Delphine Haley.

The Marine Mammals of the Northwestern Coast of North America by Charles M. Scammon.

Sea Guide to Whales of the World by Lyall Watson and Tom Ritchie.

The Sierra Club Handbook of Whales & Dolphins by Stephen Leatherwood, Randall Reeves, & Larry Foster.

Whale: Mighty Monarch of the Sea by Jacques-Yves Cousteau and Phillippe Diole.

Whales by Nigel Bonner.

Whales by E. J. Slijper.

The Year of the Whale by Victor Scheffer.

For Children

Album of Whales by Tom McGowen.

Catch a Whale by the Tail by Edward R. Ricciuti.

Sea World Book of Whales by Eve Bunting.

Whales by Helen Hoke & Valeria Pitt.

Whales by John Bonnett Wexo.

Whale Watch by Ada & Frank Graham.

Information Sources

Alaska
Alaska State Museum, Juneau
University of Alaska Museum, Fairbanks

British Columbia
Greenpeace Canada (local chapters)
Pacific National Exhibition, Vancouver
Pacific Rim National Park, Ucluelet
Vancouver Public Aquarium, Vancouver

California
American Cetacean Society, San Pedro
Cabrillo National Monument, San Diego
California Marine Mammal Center, Sausalito
Channel Islands National Park, Ventura
Greenpeace, San Francisco
Lawrence Hall of Science, Berkeley
Los Angeles Museum of Natural History
Marine Mammal Fund, San Francisco
National Heritage Museum, Dana Point
The Oceanic Society, San Francisco
Orange County Marine Institute, Dana Point
Point Reyes National Seashore
Project Jonah, San Francisco
San Diego Museum of Natural History
Scripps Institution of Oceanography, La Jolla
Steinhart Aquarium, San Francisco
The Whale Center, Oakland

Oregon
Marine Science Center, OSU, Newport
Museum of Science & Industry, Portland

Washington
National Marine Mammal Laboratory, Seattle
Pacific Marine Institute, Seattle
Seattle Aquarium, Seattle
The Whale Museum, Friday Harbor

The Gentle Art of Whalewatching

The requirements are simple: warm clothing, binoculars, camera, a picnic lunch, and patience. Add a clear, windless day and calm sea, and you're ready to join the growing ranks of enthusiasts participating in the "non-consumptive use of whales"— whalewatching. Over the next few pages you'll find guidelines for increasing your whale sightings, and your understanding of just what you're likely to see, from land or by boat. To begin, these tips will help:

1. From land, look for spouts or blows from 1″ to 1½″ below the horizon.

2. Use the Diving Diagram to time and track reappearances.

3. Overcast skies reduce glare and increase your chances for sightings.

4. Early morning hours are usually most favorable, before winds whip up whitecaps.

5. Southbound, you'll see pregnant females (often swimming alone) early in the migration, small groups of adults somewhat later, and juveniles trailing.

6. Watch especially for breaching, and the thrashing or slow surface rolling that characterize courtship and mating.

7. Northbound, watch for cow-calf pairs along the surf line or near kelp beds.

Diving Diagram

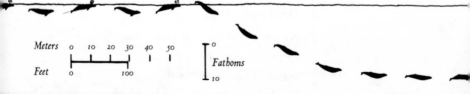

| Meters | 0 | 10 | 20 | 30 | 40 | 50 |
| Feet | 0 | | | 100 | | |

Fathoms 0 10

"Thar She Blows!"

Your first indication of the gray whale will probably be its spout or "blow"—up to 15 ft (4.5 m) high, bushy, and occasionally heart-shaped when seen from the front or rear. It will be visible for miles on calm days, and an explosive "whoosh" of exhalation may be heard up to ½ mile away. The spout consists mostly of condensation created as the whale's warm humid breath expands and cools in the sea air, along with sea water blown into the air as the whale begins its exhalation just below the surface. Look for 3-5 blows as a rule, 30-50 seconds apart before the whale dives again. (As a rule of thumb, a gray whale will blow once for each minute it has spent in its dive.) Use your stopwatch to time these blows and predict when the whale is due to blow again.

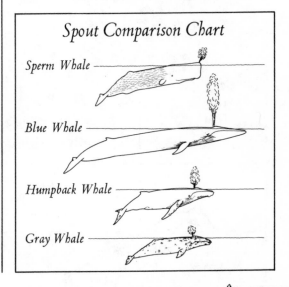

Spout Comparison Chart

Sperm Whale

Blue Whale

Humpback Whale

Gray Whale

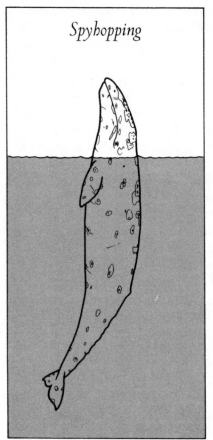

Spyhopping

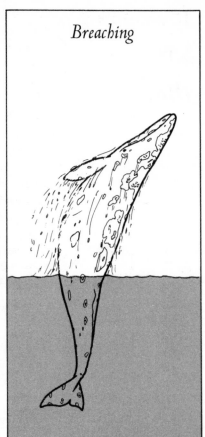

Breaching

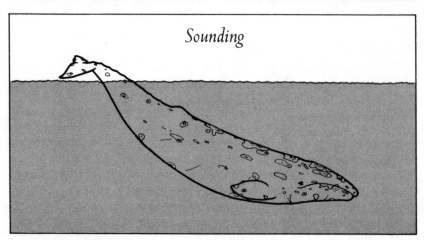

Sounding

24

Spyhopping

Gray whales are believed to have reasonable vision in air as well as water, and occasionally extend their heads vertically from the sea, to check on obstructions or simply look around. This behavior is called "spyhopping," and the sight is an extraordinary one. Supported by thrusting flukes (or, in the shallow lagoons, by resting the flukes on the bottom), the whale's head rises 8-10 feet (2-3 m) above the surface, sometimes turning slowly to scan the horizon. Thirty seconds or more may pass before it slips back under the water.

Breaching

No one knows why whales perform this most spectacular of their behaviors. It may be part of a courtship display, a signal, an effort to dislodge parasites, an expression of stress, some combination of these—or just for fun! When breaching, ¾ or more of the whale's body bursts from the water, pivots onto its side or back, and falls back with an enormous splash. Gray whales often breach two or three times in succession, and have been known to continue for a dozen or more displays.

Sounding

Following a series of short surface dives, gray whales normally descend for a single longer, deeper dive. Just before such a dive the dorsal ridge and knuckles will be readily visible. Usually the flukes appear, helping to thrust the whale's bulk into a more steeply-angled dive to get below surface turbulence. Look for the barnacles and white scars (the results of too-close encounters with killer whales, other predators, or rocks) which may mark the flukes.

Whale-watching by Boat

Excursion craft operating from seaports all along the Pacific Coast schedule regular whale-watching day trips, and offer unequalled opportunities to view gray whales from close up. Charter boats are also available for private parties. Several groups also conduct longer expeditions, a few to Alaskan waters, many more to Baja breeding lagoons.

For daytrips, be sure to take motion sickness medication *before* departure. (There appears to be no such thing as immunity to that seagoing malady!) And, in addition to the items mentioned earlier under land viewing, you'll want to bring along a raincoat. Longer expeditions will, of course, require much more gear.

In addition to the many events and behaviors observable from land, your sea-going excursion will probably introduce you to the gray whale's "footprint," that glassy-slick area of the surface left behind after a dive, or created by the powerful thrust of flukes when the whale is swimming close to the surface.

Precautions for Private Boaters

As more private boat owners track the migrating gray whales, the possibility of accident or interference increases. As a result, the governments of Canada, Mexico, and the United States have passed laws and published guidelines governing whalewatching craft. Among the common provisions are:

1. Boats must not be operated at speeds faster than the whale (or slowest whale when near a group) when paralleling and within 100 yards.

2. Boats must be operated at constant speed when paralleling and within 100 yards, and must always let the whale or whales lead!

3. Boats must never be used to separate a mother and calf (risking a perilous reminder of how gray whales came to be called "devilfish"!)

4. Boats must never be used to herd or drive whales. Boaters are advised always to approach whales from astern, overtaking gradually (which may actually encourage the whale to slow and surface out of curiosity), and maintaining constant speed. Avoid joining other boats, as the increased noise may trigger such evasive or defensive action as rapid changes in direction or speed, prolonged diving, or fluke waving. Whenever a whale exhibits such behavior, boaters are cautioned to drop well back until the animal calms, or to break off contact altogether. Failure to do so can be dangerous, as well as constituting harassment of the whales and a violation of law.

Continued enjoyment of this most rewarding activity requires not only skill and prudence on the part of boaters, but understanding of and consideration for the whales themselves.

Guide
to Listings

Listings are arranged geographically, north to south, following the migration path, and are grouped according to state or country. Each listing is numbered to be located easily on the accompanying map. Each contains the whale-watching location, directions for reaching it and, where appropriate, additional details. Timing of the migration is described at the beginning of each section, with specific comments under location listings. A boat symbol on the map indicates that there are regularly scheduled whalewatching tour boats operating from that location.

For a complete, up-to-date list of whale-watching tour and excursion operators, including addresses and phone numbers, send a stamped, self-addressed envelope to:
Sasquatch Books
1931 Second Avenue
Seattle, WA 98101

Should you be without the list and wish to locate a tour boat operator, these suggestions should prove helpful:

1. In a small town call the Tourist Information Center or drive to the harbor area and inquire in person.

2. In larger cities use the Yellow Pages. (Categories include: Environmental Associations, Fishing Parties, Museums, Ticket Agencies, Tour Operators, and Tourist Information.)

Final note: Should you know of other good whale-watching locations, we'd like to hear from you.

Whale Sighting Log

Location	Date & Time	Weather	Sea Condition	# of Whales in Group	Direction of Travel

Notes

CHUKCHI
SEA

RUSSIA

BERING STRAIT

GAMBELL
SAVOONGA

① NOME

SAINT
LAWRENCE
ISLAND

BERING
SEA

ANCHORAGE

SEWAR

HOMER

KODIAK CITY

③

KODIAK
ISLAND

②

COLD BAY
UNIMAK ISLAND

UNIMAK PASS

N

ALASKA

Alaska

1. ST. LAWRENCE ISLAND in the Bering Sea is usually a good place to see gray whales during their summer feeding. July through September are the best months, and the Island's Southwest Cape is a good observation point. The Eskimo villages of Gambell and Savoonga are on the north side of the island, which is also popular with bird watchers. There are no commercial accommodations. Arrangements should be made well in advance of your trip by making contact with a local guide. Fog, logistics, and irregular movements of the whales complicate viewing efforts. There are several commercial flights weekly from Nome to St. Lawrence Island, and whales are often seen during these flights. Contact the Nome Convention & Visitors Bureau, Box 251, Nome 99762 or your travel agent for flight information. To arrange your Island stay, write the Village Council President in either Gambell or Savoonga, Alaska 99742.

2. CAPE SARICHEF on Unimak Island in the Aleutians is a prime land observation site, since most (if not all) of the gray whale population goes through Unimak Pass on both southern and northern migrations. Unfortunately, the fall period (Nov.-Dec.) is characterized by severe storms and the spring period (Apr.-June) by fog. Furthermore, travelers should be equipped for arctic camping and aware that brown bears are prevalent. An unmaintained landing strip close to Cape Sarichef is the only access to the site. Special use permits must be applied for from the U.S. Fish & Wildlife Service, Pouch 2, Cold Bay, Alaska 99571. Plane charters may be hired at Cold Bay through Peninsula Airways.

3. KODIAK ISLAND is one of the most accessible Alaskan land areas from which to watch gray whales. November through December, and April through May are the best times, as the whales pass between the Island's Narrow Cape (on the east side) and Ugak Island. A road from Kodiak (22 miles away) goes within a half hour's walk of the Cape, which has public access. There are visitors' accommodations in the town of Kodiak and the Kodiak Chamber of Commerce will provide a list. (Zip code is 99615.) Regularly scheduled commercial planes fly to Kodiak Island from Anchorage and ferries run from Homer and Seward.

British Columbia

Queen Charlotte Islands

The Queen Charlotte Islands have their best gray whalewatching period from late April into June. The two most accessible areas are on the east side of the Islands.

1. ROSE POINT/ROSE SPIT. NE corner of Graham Island. Drive to Tow Hill Provincial Park from Masset and hike along the shore. Gray whales linger around North Beach.

2. SKIDEGATE INLET. The Sandspit area, easternmost land point on Moresby Island, is recommended. On the Graham Island side, view from front steps of the museum at Second Beach or Indian Band Council Office at village of Skidegate.

Inter-island transportation is by car ferry. Limited tourist accommodations are located at Queen Charlotte City, Sandspit, Masset, Port Clements, and Tlell; rental cars at Sandspit Airport or in the cities of Masset and Queen Charlotte. The Islands can be reached by daily plane from Vancouver or by ferry from Prince Rupert. For more information, write Tourism British Columbia, 1117 Wharf St., Victoria, B.C. v8w 2z2.

Vancouver Island

3. PACIFIC RIM NATIONAL PARK, Long Beach Unit, is the place to watch gray whales on Vancouver Island. Weather is best during the migration north (from late February to June). Recommended sites are: headlands near Schooner Cove, Quisitis Point, and Wya Point; rocks below Green Point, summit of Radar Hill, and naturalist's workshop at Wickaninnish Beach (telescopes available); and Comber's Beach (gray whales may feed in vicinity of Sea Lion Rocks). During summer months, approximately 40-50 gray whales feed along Vancouver Island's west coast. Best areas for viewing are Wickaninnish Bay and Schooner Cove.

There are tourist accommodations near Pacific Rim National Park at Tofino and Ucluelet, including private campgrounds, with public camping at the Park. The Park can be reached by bus or car on Highway 4 from Port Alberni, or by ferry from Port Alberni. Planes fly from Vancouver to Tofino Airport. For more information write: Superintendent, Pacific Rim National Park, Box 280, Ucluelet, B.C. VOR 3AO.

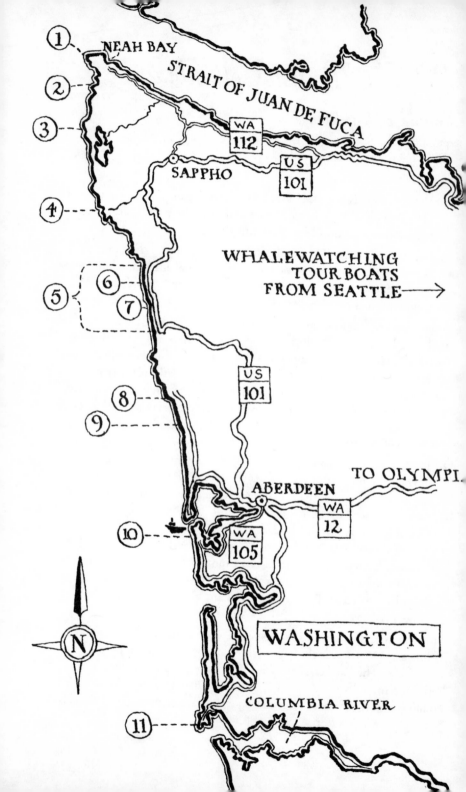

Washington has two distinct whalewatching seasons corresponding with the southern and northern migrations. During the fall period (late October through mid-December), poor weather conditions frequently preclude successful viewing (with the exception of the Cape Alava area, where observers report excellent Indian Summer sightings). The spring period (March to May) is better. Single adult whales migrate north first, with cow-calf pairs forming a second spring "pulse" through May.

Washington

1. CAPE FLATTERY. Follow Hwy. 112 west through Makah Indian Reservation, and signs to Cape Flattery. Park and walk ½ mi. to Land's End (wear boots; trail may be muddy). Also a good place to spot seals. Makah Cultural and Resource Center features Indian whaling artifacts and displays.

2. SHI SHI BEACH BLUFFS. Drive through Neah Bay toward Air Force Base; at first bridge, turn left, then stay right for 2.2 mi. Park, look for trailhead sign for Shi Shi (½ mi. walk).

3. CAPE ALAVA (FLATTERY ROCKS NATIONAL REFUGE). From Hwy. 101 turn north at Sappho to Hwy. 112; drive Hoko River Rd. to Lake Ozette; follow 4-mi. trail to Cape. Excellent viewing.

4. LA PUSH. Just north of Forks on Hwy. 101 take turnoff to La Push. Park close to road on south side of river and sit on hill to whalewatch.

5. OLYMPIC NATIONAL PARK. Hwy. 101 from Ruby Beach south to Queets has many good viewing areas.

6. DESTRUCTION ISLAND OVERLOOK. On Hwy. 101 in Olympic National Park.

7. KALALOCH. Watch outdoors or from Kalaloch Lodge library.

8. POINT GRENVILLE. Hwy. 109 on the Quinalt Indian Reservation.

9. MOCLIPS-PACIFIC BEACH AREA. On Hwy. 109.

10. WESTPORT. Use observation platforms. For information, contact Chamber of Commerce. During spring flood tides, gray whales occasionally come into harbor.

11. NORTH HEAD LIGHT (CAPE DISAPPOINTMENT). Take turnoff from Hwy. 101 toward Fort Canby State Park, then west to lighthouse. Harbor seals and sea lions also.

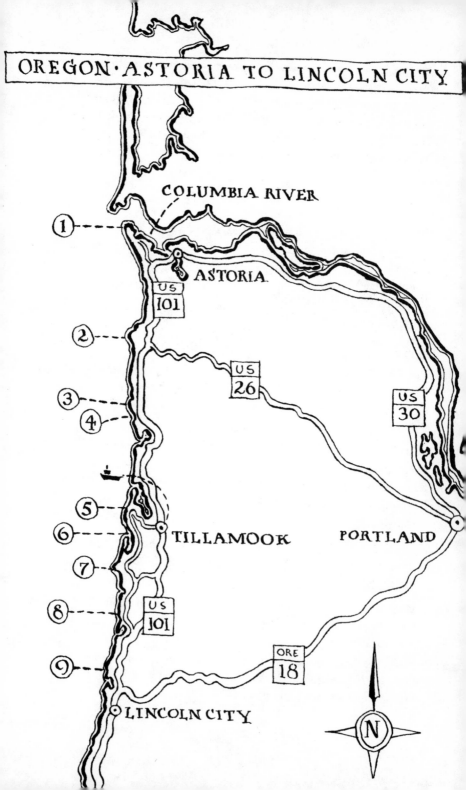

Along coastal Oregon, late December to mid-January, and mid-March through mid-May are best whalewatching times. The southern migration peaks in central Oregon at Newport between Christmas and New Year, and about a half-week later at the California border. During the northern migration, watch for two whale population "pulses," as single adults pass first, followed in late April and May by cow-calf pairs.

Oregon

[Astoria to Lincoln City]

1. FORT STEVENS STATE PARK. Two miles off Hwy. 101, west of Astoria. Whales can be seen from observation platform on south jetty.

2. TILLAMOOK HEAD (ECOLA STATE PARK). Hwy. 101 between Seaside and Cannon Beach. Follow easy hiking trail to good viewing areas.

3. CAPE FALCON (OSWALD WEST STATE PARK). Hwy. 101 south of Cannon Beach. Follow easy 1.5-2 mi. improved hiking trail to Cape.

4. NEAHKAHNIE MOUNTAIN (OSWALD WEST STATE PARK). Hwy. 101 just north of Manzanita. Climb to high areas for good viewing.

5. CAPE MEARES. West of Tillamook from Hwy. 101 on Scenic Cape Route. Drive to lighthouse. Harbor seals in Tillamook Bay.

6. SCENIC CAPE ROUTE, SOUTH OF OCEANSIDE. Good viewing from pullouts.

7. CAPE LOOKOUT. 12 mi. SW of Tillamook on Scenic Cape Route off Hwy. 101. 2-hour hike to excellent view.

8. CAPE KIWANDA. North of Pacific City on Scenic Cape Route. Road above beach has views.

9. CASCADE HEAD (SIUSLAW NATIONAL FOREST). Hwy. 101 north of Lincoln City. Use nature trail for 3-mi. hike to excellent viewing areas.

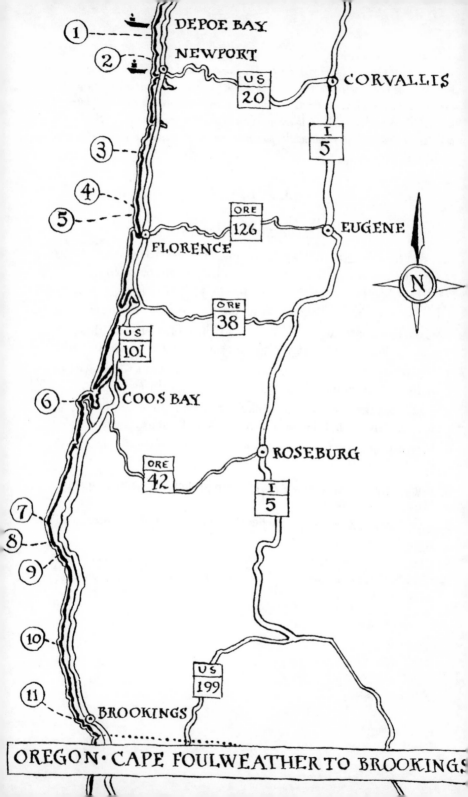

OREGON · CAPE FOULWEATHER TO BROOKINGS

Oregon

[Cape Foulweather to Brookings]

1. CAPE FOULWEATHER. Just west of Hwy. 101, 7 mi. north of Agate Beach. Especially good for viewing cow-calf migration in mid-May.

2. YAQUINA HEAD (AGATE BEACH). Drive west from Hwy. 101. (Phone Newport Chamber of Commerce to confirm road open to lighthouse.)

3. CAPE PERPETUA. 3 mi. south of Yachats on Hwy. 101. Pull off road to whalewatch, or drive into Siuslaw National Forest (pass Visitor's Information Center and take next right to parking lot for short walk to excellent viewing from bluff).

4. HECETA HEAD. Just west of Hwy. 101. Check with lighthouse caretaker for permission to use trail to bluffs.

5. SEA LION CAVES. Pull-offs on Hwy. 101 north of Caves, or park at Caves and climb hills on east side of Hwy. 101 for views from headlands. Sea lions also.

6. CAPE ARAGO (CAPE ARAGO STATE PARK). From Hwy. 101 follow signs to Charleston or Cape Arago. Parking lot overlooks reef; roads and trails go to Cape.

7. CAPE BLANCO (CAPE BLANCO STATE PARK). West off Hwy. 101 near Sixes. Drive to point for viewing near old lighthouse. Some hiking trails.

8. HWY. 101 SOUTH OF PORT ORFORD. Pull-offs from road are high and close to beach. Harbor seals at Port Orford.

9. HUMBUG MOUNTAIN STATE PARK. Hwy. 101 south of Port Orford. Strenuous hiking trails up mountain for viewing spots. Often foggy.

10. CAPE SEBASTIAN (CAPE SEBASTIAN STATE PARK). South of Gold Beach on Hwy. 101. Take hiking trail onto Cape for excellent viewing.

11. BROOKINGS. Samuel H. Boardman State Park, north on Hwy. 101. Trails to 4 or 5 good viewing spots. Also Harris Beach State Park at Brookings. Use hiking trails to areas above beach.

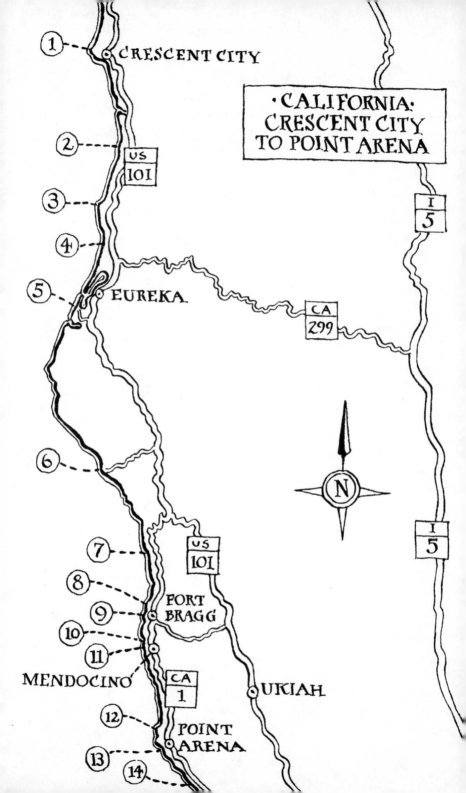

·CALIFORNIA·
CRESCENT CITY
TO POINT ARENA

In general, California's gray whalewatching season extends from early December through May. However, there is considerable variation along the 1100-mile coastline in the seasonal migratory peaks. In the northern part of the state, distinct winter (Dec.-Jan.) and spring (Feb.-May) migrations occur, the latter in two "pulses" (single adult whales followed by cow-calf pairs). In southern California, the two seasons overlap, so that at times whales heading south pass those already returning north.

California

[Crescent City to Point Arena]

1. POINT ST. GEORGE. East of Radio Rd., Crescent City.
2. PRAIRIE CREEK REDWOODS STATE PARK. West of Hwy. 101, 6.5 mi. north of Orick. Hike on high trail near Gold Bluffs Beach.
3. PATRICK'S POINT STATE PARK. 5 mi. north of Trinidad.
4. McKINLEYVILLE VISTA POINT. 2 mi. north of McKinleyville.
5. TABLE BLUFF COUNTY PARK. Table Bluff Rd. off Hookton Rd., west of Hwy. 101 at Beatrice. Watch for foggy conditions.
6. POINT DELGADA (SHELTER COVE). West on Briceland-Thorne Rd. (long and twisty) off Hwy. 101 at Redway. Becomes Shelter Cove Rd.; follow to west end.
7. WESTPORT-UNION LANDING STATE BEACH VISTA VIEWPOINTS. Hwy. 1, 15 mi. north of Fort Bragg.
8. MacKERRICHER STATE PARK. West of Hwy. 1, from Ten Mile River south to Pudding Creek, Cleone.
9. TODD'S POINT/FORT BRAGG. Just south of Noyo Bridge, go west on Ocean View Dr. from Hwy. 1. (Fort Bragg Whale Festival in March.)
10. RUSSIAN GULCH STATE PARK. West of Hwy. 1 at Russian Gulch.
11. MENDOCINO HEADLANDS STATE PARK. Seaward of Mendocino, from Lansing and Heeser Drives to Big River. Excellent whalewatching.
12. MANCHESTER STATE BEACH. From 3.5 mi. south of Alder Creek to just north of Point Arena, Manchester. Climb dunes for viewing.
13. OVERLOOKS SOUTH OF POINT ARENA. Along west side of Hwy. 1, from Schooner Gulch south for ¾ mi.
14. GUALALA HEAD (GUALALA POINT REGIONAL PARK). 1 mi. south of Gualala, Hwy. 1. Take Salal Trail to bluff.

CALIFORNIA·FORT ROSS TO CARMEL

California

[Fort Ross to Carmel]

1. SALT POINT STATE PARK. 10 mi. north of Fort Ross, Hwy. 1.
   Whalewatch talks on weekends in Jan.

2. STILLWATER COVE PARK. 3 mi. north of Fort Ross, Hwy. 1.

3. FORT ROSS STATE PARK, 10 mi. north of Jenner, Hwy. 1. '

4. JENNER. Bluffs at Eckert Acquisition (8 mi. north of Jenner, Hwy. 1)
   and at North Jenner Beaches (from Russian Gulch to Jenner).

5. BODEGA HEAD (BODEGA HEAD STATE PARK). End of Westside Rd.

6. POINT REYES NATIONAL SEASHORE. Take Sir Francis Drake Blvd.
   from Hwy. 101 to the end, or Hwy. 1 to Olema and follow signs.
   Long stairway leads to the lighthouse, a top whalewatching site.

7. MARIN HEADLANDS (GOLDEN GATE NATIONAL RECREATION AREA).
   Take Alexander Ave. exit off Hwy. 101, north of Golden Gate
   Bridge. Use Conselman Rd. to Point Bonita, or Bunker Rd. to
   Rodeo Beach. Point Bonita best for north-bound cow-calf migration.

8. CLIFF HOUSE (SAN FRANCISCO). Drive west on Geary Blvd. to ocean.
   Best for cow-calf migration. California sea lions on rocks year-round.

9. MONTARA LIGHTHOUSE. Hwy. 1 & 16th St., Montara. Best
   viewing Feb.-Apr.

10. BLUFFS ALONG HWY. 1. South of Pescadero to Pigeon Point Rd.

11. AÑO NUEVO STATE RESERVE. Off Hwy. 1 at New Year's Creek.
    Best viewing Jan., Mar., and Apr. (cows-calves). Harbor seals,
    California sea lions, and elephant seals also. Reservations necessary
    for access to elephant seal breeding area.

12. DAVENPORT BLUFFS. Along Hwy. 1, from Año Nuevo south to
    Wilder Ranch State Park.

13. POINT PINOS. Along Ocean View Blvd., NW of Lover's Point to end
    of Lighthouse Ave., west of Asilomar Ave., Pacific Grove.

14. SEVENTEEN-MILE DRIVE/CYPRESS POINT LOOKOUT. Monterey
    Peninsula between Pacific Grove and Carmel. Also California sea
    lions, harbor seals, sea otters. ($4.00/car.)

15. POINT LOBOS STATE RESERVE. West of Hwy. 1 at Riley Ranch Rd.,
    Carmel. Also California sea lions, harbor seals, sea otters.

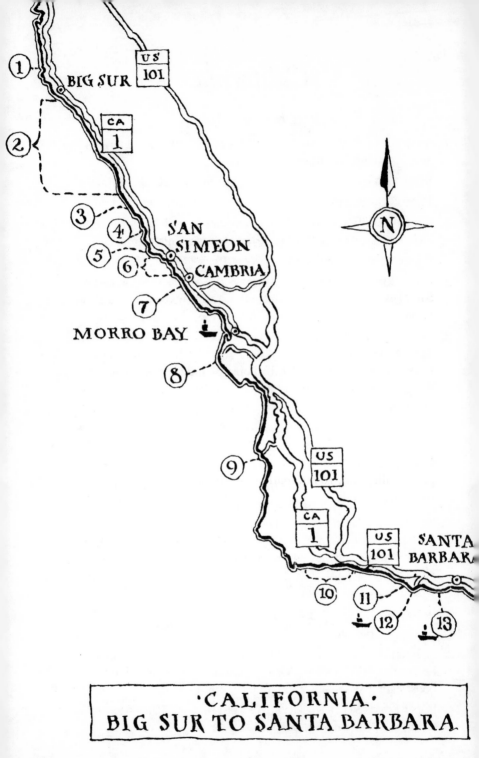

·CALIFORNIA·
BIG SUR TO SANTA BARBARA

California

[Big Sur to Santa Barbara]

1. YANKEE POINT TO POINT SUR. Cliffs along Hwy. 1. Garrapata Creek Vista Point and Bixby Creek Bridge pull-offs have fine views.

2. PFEIFFER BIG SUR STATE PARK TO RAGGED POINT. Along Hwy. 1. Whales come close at Lucia and Gorda.

3. LOS PADRES NATIONAL FOREST. Hike along Buckeye Trail for good viewing. Leave Hwy. 1 at Salmon Creek Ranger Station.

4. RAGGED POINT. West side of Hwy. 1 has good viewing.

5. POINT PIEDRAS BLANCAS. North of lighthouse, Hwy. 1 in North San Luis Obispo County. Overnight accommodations. Excellent viewing of cows-calves.

6. SAN SIMEON POINT (WILLIAM R. HEARST MEMORIAL STATE BEACH). West of Hwy. 1 on San Simeon Rd. Also overlooks south along Hwy. 1. San Simeon annual Whaling Days in November.

7. CAMBRIA. Moonstone Beach Drive Vista Point to Leffingwell Landing (north end of Moonstone Beach Dr. and Hwy. 1 to ¼ mi. south of intersection with Hwy. 1); and overlooks west of Nottingham Dr. at Plymouth & Lancaster Sts. Also sea otters at Leffingwell Landing.

8. POINT BUCHON (MONTANA DE ORO STATE PARK). South end of Pecho Valley Rd., 10 mi. south of Morro Bay.

9. POINT SAL (POINT SAL BEACH STATE PARK). End of Brown & Pt. Sal Rds., west of Guadalupe. Also California sea lions, harbor seals.

10. POINT CONCEPTION AREA. Gaviota State Park: Hwy. 101 at Gaviota Beach Rd., Gaviota. Refugio State Beach: south of Hwy. 101 at Refugio Rd., 15 mi. north of Goleta.

11. ISLA VISTA. Coastal bluffs at Isla Vista County Park, Window to the Sea Park, and Isla Vista Beach. On Del Playa Dr. Feb.-Apr. best.

12. UC SANTA BARBARA CAMPUS. Coastal bluffs. Take Clarence Ward Memorial Blvd., Goleta. Feb.-Apr. best.

13. SANTA BARBARA. Arroyo Burro Beach County Park: take Las Positas Rd. exit west off Hwy. 101, turn right at Cliff Dr. Good viewing at Henry's Beach near Brown Pelican Restaurant. Also Shoreline Park bluffs, 1200 Shoreline Dr. Feb.-Apr. best.

US
101

VENTURA
OXNARD

I
5

CA
1

LOS ANGELES

LONG BEACH

① ② ③

REDONDO BEACH

NEWPORT
BEACH

④ ⑤

⑥

⑦

⑧

⑨ ⑩

OCEANSIDE

⑪

I
5

⑫

LA JOLLA ⑬

SAN DIEGO ⑭

MEXICO

N

·CALIFORNIA·
VENTURA TO SAN DIEGO

California

[*Ventura to San Diego*]

1. CHANNEL ISLANDS. Take ferry from Ventura to Anacapa Island.

2. POINT MUGU BEACH. Bluffs at Point Mugu Rock, south of the Navy Firing Range, west side of Hwy. 1.

3. MALIBU. Leo Carrillo State Beach, 36000 block of Pacific Coast Hwy. Point Dume Whale Watch and Westward Beach Point Dume State Beach bluffs, Westward Beach Rd.

4. PALOS VERDES. Palos Verdes Estates Shoreline Preserve (west of Hwy. 1); Point Vicente County Park (Palos Verdes Dr. W., south of Hawthorne Rd.); and Marineland (6600 Palos Verdes Dr. S.).

5. SAN PEDRO. White Point at Royal Palms State Beach (Western Ave. & Paseo del Mar); Point Fermin Park (Paseo del Mar & Gaffey St.) has Cetacean & Community Building and weekend whalewatch station (free whale movie).

6. CORONA DEL MAR. Ocean Blvd. bluffs. Also south along Hwy. 1 to Irvine State Land between Arch Rock & Irvine Cove.

7. LAGUNA BEACH. Laguna Beach vista point (west end of Crescent Bay Dr.); Heisler Park (west of Cliff Dr., 400 block); and Ruby viewpoint (west end of Ruby St.). Marine life refuge offshore.

8. BLUE LANTERN LOOKOUT PARK (DANA POINT). South end of Blue Lantern St. Festival of Whales each weekend in Feb.

9. SAN CLEMENTE TO OCEANSIDE. Views from bluffs along I-5.

10. SAN ONOFRE STATE BEACH. SW of I-5, 2.5 mi. south of Basilone Rd. off-ramp, San Onofre. Hiking trails lead to whalewatching spots.

11. ENCINITAS TO DEL MAR. Coastal bluffs along Pacific Coast Hwy.

12. TORREY PINES. Torrey Pines State Reserve: west of N. Torrey Pines Rd., 2 mi. north of Genesee Ave. Glider Port at Torrey Pines City Park: west of N. Torrey Pines Rd., at end of Torrey Pines Scenic Dr.

13. POINT LA JOLLA. Coast Walk (off Torrey Pines Rd.) and viewpoints along Coast Blvd., Neptune Pl., Camino De La Costa, La Jolla Blvd., & Calumet Ave. Dec.-Feb. best.

14. CABRILLO NATIONAL MONUMENT (POINT LOMA). South end of Cabrillo Memorial Dr. Excellent viewing. Telescope-equipped whalewatching platform and glassed-in observatory. Whale programs.

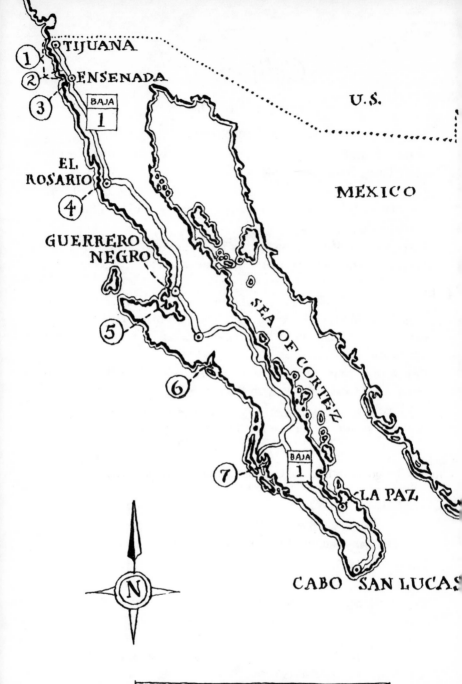

TIJUANA

ENSENADA

BAJA 1

U.S.

MEXICO

EL ROSARIO

GUERRERO NEGRO

SEA OF CORTEZ

BAJA 1

LA PAZ

CABO SAN LUCAS

N

BAJA CALIFORNIA

Gray whales begin arriving in the northern coastal waters of Baja in December, with the southern migration continuing until late February. During the latter month, most "single" whales head north, followed throughout March and April by cow-calf pairs.

Baja California

1. TIJUANA-TO-ENSENADA TOLL ROAD. Continuous viewing along bluffs.

2. EL MIRADOR TURNOFF. 20 mi. north of Ensenada, along Tijuana-to-Ensenada Toll Road. Good viewing 1000 feet above sea level.

3. PUNTA BANDA POINT. Leave Baja #1 at Maneadero (11 m. south of Ensenada), follow signs to la Bufadora, 13 mi. NW. Several good viewing spots along the road. Trailer park at la Bufadora.

4. EL ROSARIO. Take gravel road west off Baja #1 to Punta Baja. (4-wheel-drive vehicle recommended.)

5. LAGUNA OJO DE LIEBRE (SCAMMON'S LAGOON). See page 51 for map and information.

6. LAGUNA SAN IGNACIO. See page 51 for map and information.

7. BAHIA MAGDALENA. See page 51 for map and information on Estero Soledad viewing area.

Gray whales are often seen at the southern tip of Baja California in the coastal waters off Cabo Falso, Cabo San Lucas, and Bahia San Jose del Cabo. A few go north into the Gulf of California (Sea of Cortez).

Laguna Ojo de Liebre (Scammon's Lagoon) and Laguna Guerrero Negro (Black Warrior Lagoon) are just a short drive apart. No boats are allowed without special permit issued by the Mexican government; plan on whalewatching from land only. The gray whales usually begin arriving at the end of December and leave early in April. Both lagoons can be reached from the town of Guerrero Negro, to the west off Baja #1. Guerrero Negro has hotel accommodations, restaurants, a bank, and a paved trailer park with water.

1. To get to Laguna Guerrero Negro, drive through town and proceed north five miles to a small peninsula that juts out into the lagoon. Whalewatch from these abandoned salt-loading piers.

2. The turnoff to Laguna Ojo de Liebre is 4 miles south of Guerrero Negro on Baja #1 and is marked "National Park of Gray Whales." You will need a 4-wheel-drive vehicle or a pick-up with high clearance and wide tires. Camping is permitted at the Lagoon shores.

Laguna San Ignacio is difficult to reach by land. You will need a 4-wheel-drive vehicle and should not attempt the 50-mile drive from the city of San Ignacio (on Baja #1) without inquiring at the grocery store or from other local merchants whether the road is passable. It is rocky, mountainous, and traverses salt flats. If it has rained, the road may be a muddy mire. At the Lagoon you will find desert land with mud flats at low tide. Be prepared for desert camping if you wish to stay overnight. It is not as good a spot for land viewing as Guerrero Negro or Bahia Magdalena. Gray whales arrive in January and leave during April. No boats are permitted on the Lagoon without the special permit issued by the Mexican government.

Bahia Magdalena has a northern area, Estero Soledad, which affords good gray whalewatching from land. Take a bus from La Paz or drive to Puerto Lopez Mateos on the graded dirt road (turn off Route 22 approximately 15 miles west of Ciudad Constitucion). There is a fish cannery at Puerto Lopez Mateos. You can sit on the dock and watch the whales. There is also whalewatching at San Carlos. A good viewing area is near the grain elevators.